I0606419

TENNESSEE

MISSOURI
KENTUCKY
VIRGINIA
ARKANSAS
NORTH CAROLINA
MISSISSIPPI
ALABAMA
GEORGIA
TENNESSEE
NASHVILLE
L. Barkley
Clarksville
Portland
Springfield
Union City
Henderson-ville
Gallatin
Old Hickory L.
Dave Hollow Lake
Norris Lake
Clinch R.
Kingsport
Bristol
Holston R.
Elizabethton
Cumberland R.
Paris
Kentucky Lake
Mt Juliet
Lebanon
Cookeville
Cherokee L.
Morristown
Johnson City
Obion R.
Camden
Dickson
J.P. Priest L.
Oak Ridge
Clinton
Greeneville
Dyersburg
Brentwood
La Vergne
Smyrna
Douglas L.
Knoxville
Franklin
Center Hill Lake
Crossville
Farragut
Milan
Humboldt
Duck R.
Murfreesboro
Sevierville
Maryville
Spring Hill
Lexington
McMinnville
Brownsville
Jackson
Columbia
Pikeville
Watts Bar Lake
Tennessee R.
Covington
Buffalo R.
Shelbyville
Manchester
Sequatchie R.
Athens
Hatchi R.
Tennessee R.
Tullahoma
Hiwassee R.
Bartlett
Bolivar
Savannah
Lawrenceburg
Tims Ford L.
Cleveland
Memphis
Winchester
Collierville
Wolf R.
Pickwick Lake
Elk R.
Chattanooga
East Ridge

TENNESSEE

THE VOLUNTEER STATE

Jacqueline Hope Raynor

FIREFLY BOOKS

Published by Firefly Books Ltd. 2025

First Printing

Library of Congress Control Number: 2025936112

Library and Archives Canada Cataloguing in Publication
Title: Tennessee : the Volunteer State / Jacqueline Hope Raynor.
Names: Raynor, Jacqueline Hope, author.
Description: Includes index.
Identifiers: Canadiana 20250185105 | ISBN 9780228105886 (hardcover)
Subjects: LCSH: Tennessee—Guidebooks. | LCSH: Tennessee—Description and travel. | LCGFT: Guidebooks.
Classification: LCC F434.3 .R39 2025 | DDC 917.680454—dc23

Published in Canada by
Firefly Books Ltd.
50 Staples Avenue, Unit 1
Richmond Hill, Ontario
L4B 0A7

Published in the United States by
Firefly Books (U.S.) Inc.
P.O. Box 1338, Ellicott Station
Buffalo, New York
14205

Cover and interior design: Jacqueline Hope Raynor
Photo Editor: Cathy Hoshino

Printed in China | DC

INTRODUCTION

Tennessee, in the southeastern United States, is known for its rich history and cultural heritage, scenic landscapes and mountains, and thriving urban centers. With a population of just over seven million, the state balances modern city life in Nashville, Memphis, Knoxville, and Chattanooga with rural charm and Southern traditions of hospitality.

Tourism thrives in Tennessee, fueled by its world-famous music scene and scenic mountains. Nashville, nicknamed "Music City," is home to the Grand Ole Opry and the Country Music Hall of Fame. The city has launched the careers of artists like Dolly Parton, Taylor Swift, and Johnny Cash. Memphis, the birthplace of blues and rock 'n' roll, features landmarks like Graceland and Beale Street, tied to legends such as Elvis Presley, B.B. King, and Isaac Hayes.

Pigeon Forge adds to the region's appeal with family-friendly attractions, including Dollywood, one of the top 10 theme parks in the country with rides, shows, music, shopping, and dining for everyone.

The Great Smoky Mountains National Park is the most visited national park in the country and is known for its mist-covered peaks, diverse plant and animal life, and over 800 miles of hiking trails.

Historically, Tennessee played a pivotal role in the Civil War, being the last to secede and the first to rejoin the Union. The state was also central to the civil rights movement, most notably in Memphis, where Dr. Martin Luther King Jr. was assassinated in 1968. Tennessee's antebellum history is preserved in several plantation sites, such as Belle Meade in Nashville, which offer insight into the lives of enslaved people and the economic systems that shaped the region before the Civil War.

Today, Tennessee continues to attract visitors and residents alike with its mix of historic significance, educational excellence, and cultural richness. Whether enjoying mountain trails, sampling moonshine, exploring plantation sites, or taking in live music, the state offers a compelling fusion of past and present.

The Great Smoky Mountains National Park is a haven for wildlife. Black bears, the park's most famous residents, roam freely alongside white-tailed deer, wild turkeys, and the recently reintroduced elk. More elusive creatures, like bobcats and foxes, inhabit the deeper woods. The park is also a paradise for birdwatchers, with over 240 species recorded.

(Opposite) A beautiful Autumn day in Cades Cove, nestled in Great Smoky Mountains National Park. A lovely white church, one of three historic churches in the area built by early settlers, can be glimpsed through the trees.

(Previous page) Gatlinburg, a mountain resort town with a population of just over 3,500 people, is located at the edge of Great Smoky Mountains National Park. The Great Smoky is one of the most popular national parks in the country and has over 800 miles of trails, waterfalls, historic buildings, and panoramic vistas.

Jack Daniel's is one of America's most iconic whiskey brands, with deep roots in Tennessee history. Officially established in 1866 in Lynchburg, it holds the distinction of being the oldest registered distillery in the United States. Jasper "Jack" Daniel learned the craft of whiskey-making from a preacher named Dan Call and an enslaved man named Nathan "Nearest" Green. Green, who later became the distillery's first master distiller, played a vital role in its early success. The distillery was forced to shut down during Prohibition in the early 20th century and remained closed for years. Although national Prohibition ended in 1933, restrictive state laws in Tennessee delayed the reopening. Full production didn't resume until 1947, under the leadership of Jack's nephew and heir, Lem Motlow.

(Opposite) As they walk into the Visitor Center, people are met by a life-size statue of Jack Daniel himself and a full display of branded products for sale. The distillery remains one of Tennessee's top tourist attractions, with hundreds of thousands of visitors each year.

JACK DANIEL DISTILLERY
6
5
ON THE PROCESS
6 BARRELING & MELLOWING 5

Kuwohi, formerly known as Clingmans Dome, is the Cherokee name for the mountain and means "mulberry place." At 6,643 feet above sea level, it is the highest point in Tennessee and one of the tallest peaks in the Appalachian Mountains. At its summit stands a 54-foot observation tower that offers sweeping 360-degree views of the Great Smoky Mountains. On especially clear days, particularly after a cold front, visibility can stretch as far as 100 miles across seven different states. Kuwohi is a place of deep cultural significance for the Cherokee people, who consider it part of their ancestral homeland.

(Opposite) Pigeon Forge is a popular mountain resort town and the gateway to Dollywood, one of Tennessee's top tourist attractions — second only to the Great Smoky Mountains. The park features award-winning thrill rides, including the Lightning Rod and Wild Eagle (America's first wing coaster), along with a sprawling water park and a museum showcasing Dolly Parton's costumes and personal memorabilia.

MYSTERY MINE
Mystery Mine

USED
OK
CARS
USED CARS
USED
OK
CARS
DRIVE
ONE
BUY
ONE
I-ELVIS

With seating for up to 900 guests, the Showstreet Palace Theater at Dollywood hosts a variety of performances, including musical tributes, gospel concerts, and interactive shows.

(Opposite) Lightning Rod is a groundbreaking hybrid roller coaster that blends the nostalgic appeal of a wooden coaster with the cutting-edge speed and smoothness of steel. Opened in 2016 at a cost of $22 million, it reaches speeds of up to 73 mph and features a dramatic 165-foot drop at a 73-degree angle. Nearby, Rockin' Roadway offers a charming counterpoint with its 1950s-themed classic car ride in the Jukebox Junction area. Guests cruise in miniature Thunderbirds, Corvettes, or Cadillacs along twin tracks, passing nostalgic Burma-Shave-style billboards, vintage tunnels, and bridges, all set to the sound of upbeat jukebox tunes.

In the Appalachian Mountains, located in the Cherokee National Forest, a vast, scenic wilderness stretches over 650,000 acres of protected forestland. It offers the crystal-clear waters of Watauga Lake, fishing, hiking, and camping. (Opposite) Conasauga Falls is a scenic 35-foot waterfall located in the Forest, near the town of Tellico Plains; nestled along a short hiking trail, the falls offer a peaceful retreat surrounded by lush woodland and natural beauty.

Created in 2019 as part of the city's bicentennial celebrations, the huge MEMPHIS sign on Mud Island River Park has become a popular spot amongst locals and tourists alike.

(Opposite) The Hernando de Soto Bridge, connecting Memphis, Tennessee and West Memphis, Arkansas, carries Interstate 40 across the Mississippi River. Opened in 1973, the bridge's distinctive steel arches have earned it the nickname "The M Bridge."

(Following page) An aerial shot of Memphis at sunset, stretched out along the Mississippi River.

Shelby Farms Park in Memphis is one of the largest urban parks in the United States. In 2007 Shelby County combined several areas into a public park spanning 4,500 acres, leading to the expansion of Hyde Lake (formerly Patriot Lake), the creation of new trails, the construction of the Woodland Discovery Playground and the planting of over one million trees. Shelby Farms Park is also home to a thriving herd of American bison.

The National Civil Rights Museum in Memphis is dedicated to preserving and presenting the history of the Civil Rights Movement in the United States. Located in the former Lorraine Motel — the site where Dr. Martin Luther King Jr. was assassinated on April 4, 1968 — the museum offers a powerful and immersive journey through more than five centuries of African American history, from slavery to modern-day struggles for equality. Two cars, a 1959 Dodge Royal and a 1968 Cadillac, are positioned to authentically recreate the scene outside the motel as it appeared on that tragic day.

The National Civil Rights Museum also features a powerful and immersive exhibit called "The Year They Walked: Montgomery Bus Boycott 1955–1956," which centers on Rosa Parks' courageous act of defiance by refusing to move to the back of the bus and its pivotal role in igniting the Civil Rights Movement.

A. Schwab
ESTABLISHED 1876
AN ATTITUDE
ONE WAY
SPEED LIMIT 20
NO TRUCKS OR BUSES
ONE WAY
Silky O'Sullivan's
NO PARKING OR STANDING

Motorcycles crowd the street in front of the taverns and cafes on Beale Street during the weekly Biker Night.

(Opposite) Beale Street in Memphis is a vibrant cultural and musical hub, renowned for its deep roots in American music history and its lively atmosphere. Established in 1841, Beale Street quickly became a center for African American commerce and culture and, in the early 20th century, it evolved into a premier destination for blues, jazz, and R&B artists. Legendary figures like W.C. Handy, B.B. King, Louis Armstrong and Muddy Waters were regular performers and, in 1966, Beale Street was designated a National Historic Landmark.

THE LEGENDARY
SUN
Studio
MEMPHIS, TENNESSEE
SUN STUDIO
Sam Phillips
AVENUE
COME HOME TO
GRACELAND
JUST 10 MINUTES AWAY!
GRACELAND.COM
706
SUN STUDIO
Open Every Day

Unveiled in 1997, the bronze Elvis Presley statue on Beale Street depicts a young Elvis in a 1955 suit, reflecting his early days.

(Opposite) Sun Studio on Union Avenue is renowned as "The Birthplace of Rock 'n' Roll." Opened in 1950 by Sam Phillips, it became the launchpad for legendary performers such as Elvis Presley, Johnny Cash, Jerry Lee Lewis, and B.B. King. In 2003, Sun Studio was designated a National Historic Landmark.

Graceland is the iconic Memphis mansion that was home to Elvis Presley, the undisputed "King of Rock 'n' Roll." Elvis' home is now a major pilgrimage site for music fans from around the world. Bought in 1957, when Elvis was just 22 years old, Graceland was his primary residence until his death in 1977. He is buried in The Meditation Garden on the 14-acre property, alongside his parents, grandmother, and daughter, Lisa Marie Presley. Graceland became a museum in 1982 and was declared a National Historic Landmark in 2006.

Main Street is a vibrant corridor that runs from the Mississippi River through the heart of downtown Memphis. In the early 20th century, it was the city's primary commercial avenue but, by the 1950s, the area had entered a period of urban decay. In the early 2000s, investment and preservation efforts, including restoration of historic buildings like the Orpheum Theatre and National Civil Rights Museum, established the South Main Arts District as a hub for art galleries, boutique shops, restaurants, and nightlife.

The Old Daisy Theatre on Beale Street opened in 1913 and is a prime example of Nickelodeon-style architecture, characterized by its grand half-dome entrance and unique interior design. From the 1930s to the 1960s, the Old Daisy was a prominent stop on the Chitlin' Circuit, a network of venues that provided safe performance spaces for African American artists during the Era of Segregation. Legendary performers such as Aretha Franklin, Duke Ellington, Lena Horne, and Wilson Pickett graced its stage.

Opened in 1928, the Orpheum Theatre was designed in the Italian Renaissance style. The original building featured opulent interiors with brocade draperies, crystal chandeliers, gilded moldings and a Mighty Wurlitzer organ. In the 1940s the Orpheum transitioned to showing first-run movies under the name "Malco." Finally, in 1977, the Memphis Development Foundation purchased the building, restored its original name and brought Broadway shows and live performances back to the Orpheum.

The elevated roads in Memphis, especially the ones running through the downtown area, were constructed because the Mississippi River is prone to flooding. Elevating the roads helps protect them from floodwaters, ensuring that traffic can continue to flow, even during high water events. Elevated roads also help to manage increasing traffic in the downtown area, separating local traffic from interstate or through traffic.

Egrets perform a mating dance along the banks of the French Broad River, an important waterway that flows through both North Carolina and Tennessee, where it joins the Holston River in Knoxville to form the Tennessee River.

(Opposite) The Dixon Gallery and Gardens in Memphis is a fine art museum and public garden that opened in 1976 and attracts more than 30,000 visitors annually. It was established by philanthropists Hugo and Margaret Dixon who bequeathed their home, art collection, and gardens to the city. The museum boasts an impressive collection of over 2,000 works, including French and American Impressionist paintings. The Dixon's gardens are renowned for their seasonal displays, particularly the spring tulip bloom.

The Flagg Grove School in Brownsville was the one-room school attended by Tina Turner, the legendary "Queen of Rock 'n' Roll." Established in 1889 and in use until the 1960s, it served African American children. In 2014 the building was relocated to the West Tennessee Delta Heritage Center, restored and opened as the Tina Turner Museum, showcasing memorabilia from her career and honoring early African American education.

(Opposite) Completed in 1941, the Crystal Shrine Grotto in Memorial Park Cemetery in Memphis is a unique man-made cave adorned with over five tons of quartz crystals. The grotto was created by Mexican artist Dionicio Rodríguez, using wire mesh, copper tubing, and cement. Inside the grotto, there are ten dioramas depicting scenes from the life of Christ, including The Nativity, The Last Supper, The Crucifixion, and The Resurrection.

Horse farming in Tennessee has a long tradition as part of the state's rural culture and agricultural history. With its rolling hills and pastures, the state is renowned for its expertise in breeding, training and raising horses.

The Tennessee Walking Horse (above), is a breed known for its unique gait, the "running walk," which provides a smooth, comfortable ride. The breed was originally developed for farm work and transportation but gained popularity as a show horse due to its distinctive movement. Tennessee hosts the Tennessee Walking Horse National Celebration in Shelbyville, one of the largest horse shows in the world.

Pickett CCC Memorial State Park is a haven for outdoor enthusiasts and stargazers. Nestled within the upper Cumberland Mountains, the park spans over 19,000 acres and features caves, natural bridges, and sandstone bluffs. It was designated a Silver-tier Dark Sky Park in 2015 and hosts monthly star parties.

(Opposite) The Cane Creek Suspension Bridge in Fall Creek Falls State Park is approximately 150 feet long and hangs 20 feet above Cane Creek, offering beautiful views of the surrounding gorge.

(Following page) Chattanooga is a vibrant city known for its natural beauty, rich history, and revitalized downtown. It blends outdoor adventure opportunities with urban charm. Recognized for its diverse attractions and unique personality, it was named one of the South's best cities in 2025 by *Southern Living* magazine.

The Chickamauga and Chattanooga National Military Park, established by Congress in 1890, was the first park in the United States to preserve the sites of pivotal Civil War battles and to honor the soldiers who fought there. The park covers more than 9,000 acres as it stretches across Georgia and Tennessee.

Point Park (within the larger national park) offers sweeping views of Chattanooga River and the Tennessee River Valley. The Civil War Cannon Monument is located on Lookout Mountain (above). The New York Peace Memorial (opposite page), a 95-foot-tall monument, is constructed from Tennessee marble and pink Massachusetts granite. The statue at the top shows a Union and Confederate soldier shaking hands under a single flag, symbolizing reconciliation and peace between the North and South following the Civil War.

Discovered in 1928 inside Lookout Mountain, Ruby Falls is an underground waterfall that drops 145 feet down into a limestone cavern. It's one of the tallest and most beautiful underground waterfalls in the country.

Umbrella Alley is a colorful public art installation located in the heart of downtown Chattanooga. This unique alleyway features a canopy of brightly colored umbrellas suspended above the street, inviting visitors to explore the area and take photographs.

Opened in 1992, the Tennessee Aquarium, located along the scenic riverfront in Chattanooga, is home to more than 12,000 animals representing almost 800 species. The distinctive-looking building is organized vertically: two living forests, representing terrestrial habitats, are located at the top of the building and lit by skylights, while underwater habitats are viewed from the building's multistory central "canyon."

(Opposite) The Creative Discovery Museum, in downtown Chattanooga, opened its doors in 1995 to serve as a hands-on educational space for children, featuring exhibits in art, music, science, and technology.

W
E
HELP US CREATE THE NEW CDM

OTTERS!

Spanning 33 acres in the Southside district of Chattanooga, Sculpture Fields at Montague Park is an outdoor sculpture park blending art and nature. The park features over 50 large-scale sculptures created by international artists that are strategically placed along the park's 1.5 miles of trails. (Above) *Cinderella* by John Clement frames *Odyssey* by Ray Katz. *Granite Windows* by Jesus Moroles is seen to the right.

(Opposite) The Chief John Ross Bridge, commonly known as the Market Street Bridge, spans the Tennessee River and connects downtown Chattanooga with the North Shore district. Completed in 1917, it features a 310-foot double-leaf bascule lift span. In 1950 the bridge was renamed in honor of Chief John Ross, the longest-serving principal chief of the Cherokee Nation.

Perched on an 80-foot bluff overlooking the Tennessee River, the Hunter Museum of American Art offers panoramic views of downtown Chattanooga. Its collection contains over 3,000 works, spanning American art from the colonial era to contemporary pieces. The building itself is a fusion of architectural styles, reflecting its growth over the years. The Modern West Wing (opposite), juts out dramatically from the bluff edge and, with its overhanging mass, creates a sense of the building hovering above the landscape. The Williams Stairway, connecting the Hunter Museum to the Bluff View Art District, is a popular shortcut through the hills of downtown Chattanooga and provides stunning views of the surrounding area.

Ayres Hall is a historic and architectural landmark at the University of Tennessee, Knoxville. Completed in 1921, a prominent 140-foot bell tower rises above the central section, adorned with gargoyles and checkerboard brickwork.

(Opposite) Neyland Stadium is the iconic home of the University of Tennessee Volunteers football team (nicknamed the VOLS). Located on the banks of the Tennessee River, it has a seating capacity for over 100,000 fans. The stadium is named in honor of Robert Neyland who served as head coach and transformed the Volunteers into a national powerhouse that claimed four national championships and had six undefeated seasons.

NEYLAND STADIUM
HOME OF THE VOLS
VOLS

The Cathedral of the Most Sacred Heart of Jesus is the seat of the Catholic Diocese of Knoxville. The present church was completed in 2018, drawing inspiration from classical ecclesiastical architecture, most notably the Florence Cathedral. Constructed using Indiana limestone and Roman-style bricks, the building's most striking feature is the 144-foot-high dome adorned with murals depicting the Twelve Apostles and a central image of the Sacred Heart of Jesus. The cathedral boasts a 45-foot-tall *baldacchino* (canopy) over the altar (opposite page). The altar is crafted from Michelangelo Statuario marble, sourced from the same quarry as Michelangelo's *Pietà*.

ABODE OF JUSTICE AND LOVE
MOST WORTHY OF PRAISE
WORTHY IS THE LAMB THAT WAS SLAIN
BURNING FURNACE OF CHARITY

Alex Haley statue in Haley Heritage Square in Knoxville.

Alex Haley (1921–1992) was a groundbreaking American author and journalist, best known for two books: *Roots: The Saga of an American Family* and *The Autobiography of Malcolm X*. His writings profoundly influenced American history and culture, sparking widespread interest in African American history and genealogy. In recognition of his work, Haley's childhood home in Henning (opposite) was restored and opened to the public as the Alex Haley Interpretive Center, offering visitors insights into his life and work.

Alexander Murray Palmer
Haley
Author of Pulitzer Prize
winning novel "Roots".
Other Novels:
Malcolm X
Palmer Town
Madam Walker
A Different Kind Of Christmas
Queen
Henning
Fred Montgomery

The Green McAdoo Cultural Center in Clinton honors the legacy of the Clinton 12 who, in 1956, were the first African American students to desegregate a state-supported high school in the South. The building was added to the National Register of Historic Places in 2005 and was reopened as a museum in 2006 to commemorate the 50th anniversary of the Clinton 12's historic act. The life-sized bronze statue, titled *The Clinton 12 – Walking into History*, was unveiled on May 17, 2007.

The Y-12 Plant and X-10 Graphite Reactor (above) in Oak Ridge, Tennessee, were vital components of the Manhattan Project. The Y-12 Plant was built to enrich uranium using an electromagnetic process, ultimately producing the fissile material for the bomb dropped on Hiroshima. Just down the road, the X-10 Graphite Reactor became the world's first continuously operating nuclear reactor, originally designed as a pilot plant for plutonium production. Together, these facilities helped pioneer nuclear technology and marked the dawn of the atomic age. Today, both are preserved as part of the Manhattan Project National Historical Park.

The Sprocket Rocket is a 15-passenger pedal-powered party bike that offers a unique way to explore Nashville's vibrant downtown area.

(Opposite) The Nashville skyline shortly after a storm. In 19th-century Tennessee, historic steamboats like this were not only a symbol of technological innovation, a trip in their luxurious cabins became a symbol of wealth, social status, and leisure, particularly among the Southern elite.

The Country Music Hall of Fame and Museum in Nashville is dedicated to preserving and celebrating the rich history of country music. Since its opening in 1967, the museum has become one of the most visited history museums in the United States, welcoming over 1.6 million visitors a year.

(Opposite) The Tennessee State Capitol building in Nashville is a prominent example of Greek Revival architecture. Constructed between 1845 and 1859, it remains one of the oldest working state capitols in the country. Notably, it is one of the few state capitols without a dome.

The Ryman Auditorium (above) and the Grand Ole Opry House (opposite) in Nashville are two of the most iconic and historically significant music venues in the United States. The Grand Ole Opry is known as the "Home of Country Music." Founded in 1925, it began as a simple radio broadcast and grew into the longest-running radio show in American history. The Ryman Auditorium hosted the Opry from 1943 to 1974, when it moved to its current home in the Grand Ole Opry House.

Gibson
GRAND OLE OPRY
WELCOME TO THE OPRY

The Frist Art Museum is housed in Nashville's historic 1930s Art Deco former main post office building. The museum does not maintain a collection but rather presents a rotating schedule of temporary exhibitions sourced from around the world, ensuring that visitors always encounter something new.

(Opposite) Broadway Street, often referred to as Honky Tonk Highway, is Nashville's iconic musical strip, offering a blend of musical history, modern entertainment, and local culture.

the
VALENTINE
DIERKS
Live Music
Row
NASHVILLE
BOOTS
BOOT
BARN
HANG
120 SECONDS
WIN $200

Centennial Park is a 132-acre urban oasis located in the West End district of Nashville. The full-scale replica of the Parthenon, built for the 1897 Tennessee Centennial Exposition, was designed to evoke Nashville's claim to be the "Athens of the South." The building houses a museum showcasing 19th and 20th century American art and features a 42-foot-tall statue of *Athena*, the Greek goddess of wisdom and war (above). In 2025, *USA Today* ranked it one of the top five city parks in the country.

The Little Theatre is the oldest building on the Fisk University campus. Constructed as part of a hospital barracks in the early 1860s by Union forces during the Civil War, the building was known as the "Railroad Hospital." In 1873, it was moved to its current location and repurposed for educational use. The building was remodeled into a theater in 1935 and is now a part of the university's Speech and Drama Department. Notable figures such as Sidney Poitier, Cicely Tyson, and Miles Davis have performed here.

(Opposite) Fisk University is one of the most significant Historically Black Colleges and Universities in the United States. Founded in Nashville in 1866, shortly after the end of the Civil War, it has played a pivotal role in African American education, culture, and the Civil Rights Movement. Cravath Hall (opposite), formerly the Memorial Library, opened in 1930 and is home to a world-class art collection, including the Alfred Stieglitz Collection donated by Georgia O'Keeffe in 1949.

ERASTUS MILO CRAVATH MEMORIAL LIBRARY
CRAVATH HALL

The former home of President Andrew Jackson, The Hermitage is a National Historic Landmark located just east of downtown Nashville. Built in the early 19th century, the mansion is surrounded by beautiful gardens and offers visitors insights into life in the antebellum South.

Belmont Mansion, located on the Belmont University campus in Nashville, is one of the most elaborate antebellum homes in the South. The mansion was originally part of a 180-acre estate featuring elaborate gardens, a water tower, greenhouse, art gallery, gazebos, bowling alley, bath house, and zoo. Today, the mansion is owned by Belmont University and operates as a museum.

Located just 10 minutes from downtown Nashville, the 30-acre Belle Meade Plantation provides a glimpse into the region's past. Beginning as a modest log cabin in 1807, it grew into one of the South's most famous and affluent estates, particularly known for its contributions to thoroughbred horse racing. Today the Belle Meade Historic Site & Winery operates as a museum and cultural site, interpreting both the plantation's grandeur and the lives of the enslaved people who built and sustained it.

The Belle Meade Plantation's 1884 dairy building was an impressive facility that produced up to 240 pounds of butter each week. The dairy supplied fresh milk, cream, cheese, and butter to the estate. Today, the dairy is an historical site providing valuable insights into the agricultural economy of the past.

The Music City Center, in the heart of downtown, is Nashville's central convention and exhibition facility. This 2.1-million-square-foot venue was designed to host large-scale conventions and events. Its design incorporates sustainable elements such as a four-acre green roof, solar panels, and a rainwater collection system used for irrigation.

Opened in 1996, the Bridgestone Arena, located in downtown Nashville, has become a cornerstone of Nashville's vibrant entertainment scene. Since 1998 the arena has been the home of the National Hockey League's Nashville Predators and is affectionately known as "Smashville" by its passionate fan base. In addition to hockey, and with a seating capacity of up to 20,000 for concerts, the arena has hosted performances by global superstars such as Lady Gaga, Paul McCartney, Garth Brooks, Elton John, and the Rolling Stones.

Founded in 1873, Vanderbilt University is a prestigious private research university in Nashville. It spans a 330-acre, park-like campus in the heart of the city, blending historic architecture with cutting-edge facilities.

(Above) With its magnificent rotunda, Wyatt Center is the largest and grandest building on the Peabody College campus (officially the Vanderbilt Peabody College of Education and Human Development). It is located on its own campus just southeast of Vanderbilt University's main campus in midtown Nashville. Originally built in 1914–15, the building underwent extensive renovations in the mid 1990s and has been transformed into a state-of-the-art teaching and learning center for education and human development students and faculty.

(Opposite) Completed in 2021, the 306-foot-tall, 20-story West End Tower quickly became a campus landmark and is one of Nashville's tallest residential buildings. It houses students, visiting faculty and university guests as well as conference spaces.

The Gaylord Opryland Resort and Convention Center in Nashville is one of the largest hotels in the country. Spanning nine acres, the resort features lush indoor gardens, winding pathways, and cascading waterfalls.

(Opposite) The Music Row Roundabout, also known as Buddy Killen Circle, features the *Musica* sculpture (created by Alan LeQuire, a Nashville native). Unveiled in 2003, *Musica* is the largest bronze sculpture group in the United States. Depicting nine nude figures dancing in a circle, the artwork pays homage to Nashville's rich musical heritage and serves as a centerpiece for the vibrant Music Row district.

Shiloh National Military Park (above and opposite page) preserves the site of the Battle of Shiloh, one of the most crucial early battles of the Civil War. The battle was fought on April 6–7, 1862, in Hardin County and resulted in over 23,000 casualties.

Tennessee was a border state with divided loyalties and both Union and Confederate forces drew from its population. The *Passing of Honor* monument (above) commemorates the sacrifice of Tennessee soldiers during the war; unveiled in 2005, this statue is the first major addition to the park since 1917.

(Following page) The Great Smoky Mountains National Park is a vast and ecologically rich wilderness area, covering just over 275,000 acres and straddling the border between eastern Tennessee and western North Carolina. Designated a UNESCO World Heritage Site in 1983, the park is renowned for its exceptional biodiversity.

PHOTO CREDITS

ALAMY

Rainer Lesniewski: 2; CNMages: 11; Allen Brown: 13; Ron Buskirk: 14; The Commercial Appeal/ZUMApress.com: 25; Dennis MacDonald: 36; Bonita Cheshier: 38; Dee Browning: 39; Juniors Bildarchiv GmbH: 43; Bryant Crosby: 44; Castle Light Images: 58; Don Smetzer: 62; Randy Duchaine: 63–64; Castle Light Images: 65; Jennifer Wright: 79; Images-USA: 82; Mira: 84; J. Carlee Adams: 88; Carmen K. Sisson/Cloudybright: 90–91

iSTOCK

Wirestock: 60; csfotoimages: 78; SeanPavonePhoto: 92–93

SHUTTERSTOCK

Kevin Ruck: 6–7; Ben McMurtray: 8; Dean Fikar: 9; Paul McKinnon: 10; BlueBarronPhoto: 12; Ritu Manoj Jethani: 15; Jon Bilous: 16; Flowbetta: 17; Nina Alizada: 18; dbiermanphotog: 19; Marcus E Jones: 20–21; James Kirkikis: 22; Nina Alizada: 23; DWBMedias: 24; EQRoy: 26; Gino Santa Maria: 27; dbiermanphotog: 28; James Kirkikis: 29; William A. Morgan: 30; Photo Spirit: 31; jejim: 32; Connor D. Ryan: 33; Nina Alizada: 34–35; Sean Pavone: 37; Cheri Alguire: 40; Nina Alizada: 41; AHoltPhoto: 42; VioletSkyAdventures: 45; Kevin Ruck: 46–47; Paul Brady Photography: 48; Kevin Ruck: 49; Robert Harding Video: 50; MMTravelShots: 51; Deron Levy: 52; J. Michael Jones: 53; createthis: 54; Marcus E Jones: 55; Nicholas Lamontanaro: 56; Michael Carni: 57; Grindstone Media Group: 59; Nagel Photography: 61; Claire Salvail Photos: 66; 2Kahns Photo Arts: 67; Paul McKinnon: 68; jdross75: 69; Randy Runtsch: 70; Sean Pavone: 71; RozenskiP: 72; Grindstone Media Group: 73; Chad Robertson Media: 74; 4kclips: 75; Tiphanie Brooke Johnston: 76; Fotoluminate LLC: 77; Michael Gordon: 80; Steve Heap: 81; Ryan_hoel: 83; Joseph Hendrickson: 85; Grindstone Media Group: 86; EQRoy: 87; Alexey Stiop: 89: Little Vignettes Photo: 96

INDEX

Dolly Parton was born on January 19, 1946, in a one-room cabin on the banks of the Little Pigeon River, near Sevierville. Located on the lawn of the County Courthouse, this bronze statue honors the town's most famous citizen.